WHAT'S STOPPING YOU?

MARK HOPKINS

authorHOUSE°

AuthorHouse™
1663 Liberty Drive
Bloomington, IN 47403
www.authorhouse.com
Phone: 1 (800) 839-8640

Published by AuthorHouse 05/24/2019

ISBN: 978-1-5462-4961-0 (sc)
ISBN: 978-1-5462-4960-3 (e)

Library of Congress Control Number: 2018908060

Print information available on the last page.

*Any people depicted in stock imagery provided by Getty Images are models,
and such images are being used for illustrative purposes only.
Certain stock imagery © Getty Images.*

This book is printed on acid-free paper.

*Because of the dynamic nature of the Internet, any web addresses or links contained in
this book may have changed since publication and may no longer be valid. The views
expressed in this work are solely those of the author and do not necessarily reflect the
views of the publisher, and the publisher hereby disclaims any responsibility for them.*

CONTENTS

CONTENTS

INTRODUCTION

As I sit here in the dining room of my home just reminiscing of what God has brought me through to where I am today. It has been a long road with many different life experiences that has shaped who I am today.

Born in Cleveland Ohio to George and Agnes Hopkins. Both who were born again Christians who were living for God. And at an early age, around 9 or 10, we moved to Fort Wayne, IN where I spent my childhood.

I was always thinking ahead when I was young, I knew there was something I was suppose to do, I just didn't know what. I remember at the age of 13. One day, instead of doing work at my desk in school, I was looking at a magazine and came across a page with a signup sheet for the United States Marine Corp, and while I was sitting there, I filled it out and later mailed it in. About a few weeks later, I received a letter from a 4 Star Gen stating that he would love to take me but unfortunately I was too young, and when I get 18 years old to go see my nearest recruiter. Needless to say, when I turned 18, that's what I did.

Fast forwarding, I spent four years in Active Marine Corp., three years in Marine Corp Reserves, and three years in California Army National Guard. I lived in Sacramento, CA for about thirteen years and now going on about thirteen years in Chicago, IL, where I live now. I relocated to Chicago, IL to get closer to home.

I have had lots of losses as well as gains throughout the years. There have been many things that I wanted to do. Some I've completed and some I have not, I've found that most of the things that I have not completed, there was something in common in each one of those things that stopped me from moving forward. Fear of the unknown was the thing that was constantly showing up for me.

Moving forward, this was the question that I was always asking myself. And I had to work on defeating that thing, as I am still working on just that.

I felt, that if I am having these issues I know that there are others having the same issues. So, God led me to start writing this book.

PREFACE

S ometimes we have ideas that are excellent ideas and they never go any further then being the ideas. We set them on a shelf, and every now and then, we take the idea off the shelf, dust it off, and put it right back on the shelf.

WHAT's STOPPING YOU is a book that helps you discover the things that stops you in life from becoming the person that you are striving to become or from achieving that thing in life that you want to achieve. WHAT'S STOPPING YOU, open your eyes to devices that may stop you from moving forward, and it adds some simple solutions that may help you move closer to your goals. Please, take your time reading this book, and I pray that you enjoy it.

My prayer is that you enjoy it as much as I enjoyed writing it, and that it edifies and motivates you on your process in becoming a better you.

WHAT'S STOPPING YOU, was written based on my personal experience that I have experienced throughout my life. This book may be a great road map of help to those that read it.

CHAPTER 1
Who are you?

⌒⋎⌒

The first question you need to answer is Who Are You? This question is very important to answer. You need to be very sincere about the answer so that you know exactly who you are and where you're starting from. Think about it, we all have a starting point. How determine of a person are you? When people tell you that you can't, do you believe them or do you say just the opposite, "That I can"? When you fail at something, do you take it as a failure or do you look at the positive side of it. Once being that you've learned something in your first attempt, that can help you to move further the next time. A failed attempt gives you the opportunity to start building good character. It give you the chance to perfect your _can do_ attitude, that _never give up_ attitude. Succeeding the first time you try something is great, although it really says a lot about you when you fail and continue to try and eventually succeed. It shows how determine you are to succeed at what your wanting to accomplish. Who are you? I ask that question again, do you give up at the first sign of adversity that comes your way, or do you stare your adversities directly in the face and push through them. Knowing that there is great resistance between you and your goal, although you continue to push and eventually break through the resistance. We all have some resistance in our life. At every level of life, there is some form of resistance and I must say some resistance is necessary for us, and helps us with positive growth in life. Let's answer this question. What is resistance? Resistance is anything that stops or slows down your forward progress or movement. We all deal with this at every stage of our lives, from a baby to maturity. When a baby tries to crawl or walk, and their arms and legs are not strong enough yet, they face the resistance that comes with that. They continue to fall, but after numerous attempts and with the strength that develops from trying, eventually, they learn to walk without falling. The key was that the baby continued to try not because the baby was determined to walk, but because it was natural instinct in the baby to keep trying. We all need that same kind of instinct that the baby has, to continue trying in spite of all odds. Overcoming each obstacle that comes in front of us. Learn to be determined to succeed and take the necessary steps to become that person that you want to be. You can accomplish it, nothing is stopping you but you. We need to get ourselves out of the way sometime. 90% of the battle is getting us to begin, and the other 10% is doing. If we could get ourselves out of the way we would be further in life then we are today. Think on the question asked early in this chapter, "Who Are You?"

Learn to develop good character, practice it daily, as the Bible says a good name is better than fine gold, develop good character and hold yourself to it, develop good standards, and live by them. Don't be swade to compromise the standard that you believe in. You have to stand firm, as the old saying goes, if you don't stand for something you will fall for anything. Don't allow others to dictate who you are going to be. Sometimes we can allow others to form us based on their actions toward us, because of something they did to us, we allow things to make us angry, and sometimes we continue to hold onto that anger, which can cause a lot of issues in us. That anger can cause you to become bitter, give you an unforgiving heart, which keeps you in bondage, not the other person. That person have forgot about you and moved on, while you still carrying around the hurt and the anger, which now have you trapped in that place. Release yourself by releasing the person, allowing you to move on with no animosity. You can forgive without forgetting. Don't compromise who you are, it's easier to maintain what you have then to get back what you've lost. Take fitness for instance. When I was in the United States Marine Corp we worked out every day. We ran 3 miles a day, as well as pushups, sit ups, and many other types of exercises. At that time, I believe, I only had about 10% body fat. Although, when I got out of my focus, I did not remain on physical fitness and I was able to see how quickly I began to lose the fitness that I had. Now, I'm at the point where I'm working on getting back what I lost. It would have been easier to continue with the fitness program that I already was accustomed to, then trying to redevelop the habit of working out. Form good habits to continue to develop good character. As Proverbs 22:1 KJV states, "A good name is rather to be chosen than great riches, and loving favor rather than silver and gold." If you read the 37th chapter of Genesis, you will see where Joseph's good name & favor brought him before mighty men and placed in the most important job in the country.

Stand firm to who you are and know that because of your good diligence, you will receive favor. Again, I ask you! Who are you?

Spiritual Reflection

SCRIPTURE

Matthew 5:14 – Ye are the light of the world, a city that is set on a hill that cannot be hid.

REFLECTION

Let God lead you, and be the example for others to follow. Many are looking to others for direction, be that light that will illuminate the path for others that may make their walk a little easier.

SCRIPTURE

Jeremiah 1:5 – Before I formed thee in the belly I knew thee; and before thou came forth out of the womb I sanctified thee, and I ordained thee a prophet unto the nations.

REFLECTION

God knows who you are and who He created you to be. Get a relationship with the Creator. And when you're looking for direction "ask Him for direction" and He will direct you. No one knows YOU BETTER THEN THE ONE WHO CREATED YOU!

CHAPTER 2

Who Do You Desire to Become?

N ow that you have answered the question "Who Are You," now take time to determine who do you want to become?

You need to know who you want to become in your life, in order to achieve it. What are you passionate about? At the end of your life where would you like to be? What would you have like to have accomplished? These questions can help you determine who you want to become. We have a lot of choices in life to become whomever we want, sometimes we tend to want to become too many things, at one time. Becoming one thing in life takes a lot of determination; it's even much harder when we are trying different things. We need to learn to perfect the one thing before moving to the next. Ask yourself, would you be satisfied with being the person that you want to be. And is this something you can do for the rest of your life. At the time of your death will you be okay with the person you have become? Sometimes, we go through life with no aspirations, "with no desire for achievement". And there may be invalid reasons that have us living with no desire to achieve. Some may feel that they can't do anything, some may feel that where they are is the best they can do, and some may simply believe that it's not for them. I believe deep down we all want to achieve in some form or another, and I also believe that we all can achieve what we desire to achieve. In order to achieve, we have to have the picture of what the results will be after achieving. What are the results that you are looking for? Is there a picture of the results that you have, which will confirm that you have achieved what you are trying to achieve? If you don't have the picture of the results that you are looking for, take the time to really think about it and make the decision to choose the result that you want and work to become the person you want to be.

Choosing your destination is the first step in achieving your goal, many times when I was in the Marine Corp we would be in different types of vegetation, our assignment would be to go from our camp out and complete reconnizance on an area. A lot of times, we would be in very thick vegetation and it would be very easy to get lost, the first thing we did was orientate ourselves. We would determine where we were on the map, and next where we were going and from that information, we had to plan out how to get to where we were going and how long it was going to take.

We used a compass and a map to get our Azmidth and direction from where we started from, and also plan the back Azmidth to get us back home when it was time. In thick brush you can find yourself lost and needing assistance, when you're out there, I believe life is the same way. In the 1st chapter, you answered the question who are you? That would be the same as us looking at the map and determining where we were. In this chapter, you asked, who do you want to be? Again, on the map, this would be in correlation to where are you going. In order to complete the trip successfully, you need the answer to both of these questions, in order to achieve your goal, you need the answer to both questions as well, don't lose sight of your destination. Remember, this is your story, and you're doing the writing; remember how easy it was to get lost while you're in the thick brush. In the jungle with lots of trees, bushes with no light, just wearing what we call "NVG's" (Night Vision Goggles). They didn't make very bright light, just light enough to kind of see the area you're in. Life has these same problems that you encounter along the way and you'll find yourself getting lost sometimes, remember where you came from and where you are going.

Spiritual Reflection

JUST THIS ONCE

Psalm 37:4-5 (KJV)

4 Delight thyself also in the Lord; and He shall give thee the desires of thy heart.

5 Commit thy way unto the Lord; trust also in Him; and He shall bring it to pass.

REFLECTION

Take pleasure in spending time with the Lord, when you delight in something, you enjoy being around it. You enjoy eating it. It is something that makes you happy. Learn to live the way the Lord would have you and he will bring your desires to past.

CHAPTER 3

Write the Book

Habakkuk 2:2-4 KJV states: (2) And the Lord answered me, and said, write the vision, and make it plain upon the tables, that he may run that readeth it.

(3) For the vision is yet for an appointed time, but at the end it shall speak, and not lie: though it tarry, wait for it; because it will surely come, it will not tarry.

(4) Behold, his soul which is lifted up is not upright in Him; <u>but the just shall live by his faith</u>.

Write your book, start at the first page, the first page is where you are right now in life, write them down as goals, start with daily goals. Write down the steps that you will have to make daily that moves you in the direction of who you want to be. And after completing some of the steps (and the reason I say some of the steps) is because you may not complete all the steps, just keep writing those goals down and work to complete them. You are the author of your book, your book can end anyway that you want it to end, take the time out of your life to write the pages. We deal with many distractions that change our course/ direction daily. We are changing directions so much that sometime we can even get lost within the day, and before you know it, you have not completed anything that relates to your goal or purpose. Stay on course, stay in the plan, and continue to move at a pace that allows you to complete your goals for each day. Remember <u>write the vision & make it plain, and abide therein.</u>

Spiritual Reflection

Habakkuk 2:2-3 (KJV)

2 And the Lord answered me, and said, write the vision, and make it plain upon tables that he may know that readeth it.

3 For the vision is yet for an appointed time, but at the end it shall speak, and not lie: though it tarry, wait for it; because it will surely come, it will not tarry.

REFLECTION

– Your vision will come to pass at the appointed time, write it down and make it plain. If God gave you the desire, He will give you the provision to walk in it. Believe that it will come to pass, if God said it, "IT WILL."

CHAPTER 4
What's Stopping You

We all have reason or things that stop us from reaching our goals. We have to identify what those reasons are. I like to tell people to think of 3 things that are normally there when you find yourself not accomplishing your goals, or just sitting them on a shelf collecting dust. There is always something there, and it's usually the same thing, for instance "fear." Fear plays a big role in why people delay or just plainly don't reach their goal. Fear is paralyzing, fear will stop you from even trying, and cause you to be afraid of the unknown, not knowing what will be the outcome of moving into your destiny. There are many reasons why we do not move forward in reaching our goals.

A big one for me was and sometimes was insecurity. This insecurity was not with who I am, it was more of accomplishing an unknown task, not knowing if I could accomplish the task or worrying about all the mistakes I would make. A lot of times this caused me to take more time in order to complete the task. I suppose fear also played a big role in mine as well. Think of three things that are in common with you. What is the thing that's always present when you find yourself procrastinating, is it insecurity, is it fear, is it unbelief, is it lack of courage, is it your education level, and is it because you don't have the knowledge of the task, what is it, take the time to identify those things and expose them. In order to fix the problem, you first have to expose the problem.

Spiritual Reflection

Mark 9:23 (KJV)

Jesus said unto Him, if thou can believe, all things are possible to him that believeth.

SCRIPTURE

Philippians 4:13 (KJV)

I can do all things through Christ which strengthened me.

SCRIPTURE

Jeremiah 29:11

For I know the thoughts that I think toward you, saith the Lord, thoughts of peace, and not of evil, to give you an expected end.

REFLECTION

Believe, if God gave you the desire within you to complete the task that you desire to accomplish, he has giving you the ability to succeed at it. We have to remember that we are not working off of our own strength. With our own strength some things are possible although with the strength of Christ all things are possible. When you are in God's will and being led by God, He will bring you to your expected end, which is your destiny.

CHAPTER 5

Move Forward

N ow that you have identified and exposed the things that have been stopping you from moving forward on your goals, challenge yourself to move forward past each obstacle. If its fear, move forward. If its unbelief, move forward. Believe in yourself. There is nobody better than you to complete the task, believe that you are the best person for the job, you are the best person for the position, believe that everyone needs what you have to offer, believe in yourself. You are the best person for the job and you are the best person for the business. Keep your focus on the direction that you are going and continue to move into your destiny. Overcome every obstacle that is within you that stops you from moving forward. Each time you overcome an obstacle, it becomes easier to overcome them. Before you know it, you will not have those blockages anymore. Move forward in faith. Hebrews 11:1 states, Now faith is the substance of things hoped for, the evidence of things not seen. With faith, believe and know that you will accomplish each and everyone of your goals, believe it, receive it & move in it.

Spiritual Reflection

SCRIPTURE

Philippians 3:13-14

13 Brethren, I count not myself to have apprehended: but this one thing I do, forgetting those things which are behind, and reaching forth unto those things which are before.

14 I press toward the mark for the prize of the high calling of God in Christ Jesus.

REFLECTION

- Don't let the things of the past stop your forward progress into your father. All of your short-comings, mistakes, or places where you plainly just fell short. Learn from them, but keep moving in what God has for you.

CHAPTER 6
Don't Look Back

W e often want to look back to where we came from and often want to go back, because we are more comfortable with moving into something that we are aware of. We tend to hesitate going into the unknown. Sometimes we look for every excuse to stop ourselves from moving forward into the unknown. We tend to want to stay in the condition that we are accustomed to. Sometimes we say we want more, but we are often afraid to move forward. The fear of moving forward, have us looking back to what we believe is safe. It's been working for me this far, why change now, is what we make ourselves believe, and accept. We often tell ourselves that it's easier for me in the condition that I'm in, I do not have to take any risk, because I know this area of my life so well, or if I go back to where I was, then I will be accepted and will not be required to change. I won't be judged by anyone. No one is looking for me to improve myself. The unknown can be very scary, or even downright frightening. You don't know how it's going to end. If you're going to fail or succeed, what happens if you succeed, then there are more goals and obstacles that you must overcome? In order to stay at the level, do not let your fear of moving forward draw you to go back because of the sacrifices that you are making to move forward into your unknown. Making the sacrifices will pay off in the end.

Spiritual Reflection

SCRIPTURE

Luke 9:62

And Jesus said unto him, no man, having put his hand to the plow, and looking back, is fit for the kingdom of God.

REFLECTION

This scripture is clearly referring to someone who puts their hand to the plow of ministry and working for God. I'm relating this verse to motivate you to not look back, because there will be many opportunities that will try to cause you to look back. Stay focus on what God has for you.

CHAPTER 7
Stand Firm

⌘

S tand firm as you go through your unknown. This is where you will receive a lot of your learning and information. You may even make a lot of mistakes at this time but just know that the mistakes that you are making are a part of the learning process. You may feel that the objective that you are pursuing is not for you because you don't have all the right answers, remember, no one has all the right answers. God is the only one that has all the right answers. You're going to make mistakes. I once heard a long time ago the saying, "If you are not making any mistakes, you are not doing anything." Make your mistakes, but learn from them. Our mistakes can sometimes cause us to want to give up, and stop trying. Although, I often say that we learn more from our mistakes. Of course, we do not want to make the mistakes and we do our best not to make any, but mistakes will happen. This is why you must stand firm at this time, because you can allow doubt & fear to creep in, and with the mistakes, you will be afraid to move forward. Stand firm, learn the process, find the pitfalls and learn how to maneuver around the pitfalls on your way to your destination. Hang in there, stand firm and do not give up. Continue to do the things that are moving you closer to your destination. Remember, it's like a buried treasure and you are at the right spot, you just have to keep digging and eventually you will uncover the treasure. You have to have patience while you dig, endurance, and most of all "faith".

1) You must have the patience to dig until the treasure is revealed, if you don't have the patience, you will quit before you receive the treasure.

2) You must have the endurance to keep digging without giving up because you're not able to dig anymore. Position yourself. The old story about the rabbit & the Tortoise holds truth. In the race, the rabbit took off very fast and burnt itself out and the slow tortoise came at its steady pace and passed by the rabbit and won the race. Don't burn yourself out, have the endurance to keep digging, to keep moving toward your goal until you reach your goal.

3) You must have the faith to know that the treasure is there. Hebrews 11:1 states: Now faith is the substance of things hoped for, the evidence of the things not seen. The substance means the

material in the natural realm. In spiritual aspect, substance isn't material. The substance is the part of the treasure that you can touch, can hold onto. When you're talking spiritual, it's as if the treasure is already in your hand. It's yours and you possess it already. Its like, when I go to my favorite restaurant, for my favorite food that I have a taste for. Sometimes I can taste the food even before I receive it. Through faith, I already have the food; it's mine, 'IT' hasn't shown up yet, but it's mine.

And the second part of faith is the evidence of the things not seen. The evidence is the proof, with faith being the substance. The material thing that you're hoping for is the substance. Faith is also the evidence of that material thing. Since you have the <u>substance</u> in your hand, which is the faith, means you also have the evidence in your hand as well. So as long as you have faith, the thing that you are hoping for is in your hand. It's already yours. So stand firm and don't give up. What you are hoping for is in your hand.

Spiritual Reflection

SCRIPTURE

Galatians 5:1

Stand fast therefore in the liberty where with Christ hath made us free, and be not entangled again with the yoke of bondage.

REFLECTION

Stand firm in the good work that Christ have given you. Do not allow problems and other issues to cause you to be moved from the purpose that God has instructed you to perform.

CHAPTER 8

Rocky Roads Don't Last

ᴄ*ₘ*

lthough it has been a rocky road and you have been standing firm through it all, remember rocky roads don't last, they are for a set time. Once you go through all the bumps and bruises, the learning, the mistakes, all the pitfalls, get up and dust yourself off and keep going. You'll find that you went through all that for your preparation and now that you have went through the preparation, you'll find that it is easier. You will always have those rocky roads at every stage that you go through & the bright side to this is once you go through each stage you will be collecting knowledge as you go. Overcome every obstacle as it comes your way, and before you know, you will notice that the obstacles will start repeating themselves. This is where the rocky road becomes easier because you went through the obstacle, you are better equip the second time around. You've seen the mistakes, and you've made the mistake, you know how to get around the obstacles. Now, you can also be a help to someone else who is on the same journey, someone who do not have the same life experience as you. At this point, you will notice that you feel even more confident with yourself. Remember, every challenge will have the same rocky road, but also remember that the rocky road will not last. Get on the road, move forward, and tackle every obstacle that comes your way. That rocky road will eventually become smooth.

Spiritual Reflection

SCRIPTURE

Roman 8:28 (KJV)

And we know that all things work together for good to them that love God, to them who are called according to His purpose.

REFLECTION

Every mistake, every pitfall, every trail you go through on your journey will work together for your good, as long as you continue to allow God to guild you into the purpose that He has called you to.

CHAPTER 9

Better Streets Ahead

lthough you have been on rocky roads, you did not give up, you took everything that was thrown your way. You've learned where all the pitfalls and the pot holes are. You have became a person that is more aware, more knowledgeable, more wiser, and better equipped to make more solid decisions in your field of expertise. Every bump, hole & mountain that you had to go around, through or climb, was there to help you progress and to equip you with the experience you needed to get you to the next level in your life. God doesn't leave us without the knowledge and the understanding that we need. Understanding is very important in our growth.

To grow without understanding can leave you without the tools to sustain you and may cause you to have to repeat phases in life, or it may stop you from progressing altogether. Proverbs 4:5-8 KJV states: 5. Get wisdom, gets understanding; forget it not; neither decline from the words of my mouth. 6. Forsake her not, and she shall preserve thee; love her, and she shall keep thee. 7. Wisdom is the principal thing, therefore, get wisdom and with all thy getting, get understanding. 8. Exalt her, and she shall promote thee; she shall bring thee to honor; when dost embrace her.

Use the wisdom, knowledge and the understanding that God has given and invested in you, allow God to continue to pour & invest in you and all your decisions, you cannot go wrong when following the directions of God. We all have to grow through training very often, in order to grow, we have to go through things that we've never done before. When I went into the United States Marine Corp back in 1986, the day I went to boot camp, I was flown out to San Diego, CA and I arrived at the airport, at about twelve-thirty to one o'clock in the morning, and the Marine Corp bus came to pick us up. There had to be about 30 other men waiting for the bus as well, but when the bus pulled up, and the drill instructor came off the bus, I know my life was about to change. At that moment in time, I was not in charge of myself anymore. I had to give up the control to someone else. I didn't know what to expect or how to get there. All my desire of wanting to control the things in my life was gone and given to the drill instructor. In order for me to achieve and be successful as a marine, I had to be guided by someone who was already a marine and I had to accept the guidance. By putting down my pride and accepting the guidance, I was able to go in and become the United States Marine, and that is something I am proud of myself up into this very day. We have to do the same thing with God, let go of our pride and allow God to instruct, teach and mature us in this thing called life and in every area that God is moving us into. When we allow God to direct us, we will receive all the knowledge, wisdom & understanding that we need to move forward, and by receiving this you will truly have better streets ahead.

Spiritual Reflection

SCRIPTURE

1 Corinthians 2:9 (KJV)

But as it is written, eye hath not seen, nor ear heard, neither have entered into the heart of man, the things which God hath prepared for them that love Him.

REFLECTION

There is no imaginable limitations to what God has for us, God know the plans that He has for us. His plan is to bring us to an expected end, an end with joy and peace. Continue to love God and make Him first in your life, and you will reap your reward.

CHAPTER 10

At Last

M atthew 19:26 KJV: states, "But Jesus beheld them, and said unto them, with men this is impossible; but with God all things are possible." Although this was an illustration from Jesus to the disciples about how hard it is for a rich man to enter heaven. In verse 24, Jesus stated, "It was easier for a camel to go through the eye of a needle, than a rich man to make it into the kingdom of heaven". In verse 25, the disciples questioned Jesus because of not understanding who could be saved. In verse 26, Jesus stated, without God "No One", but with God "All Is Possible", even with the rich man he can make it in with no problem. A lot of people may have counted you out, expected you to give up and fail, but with the determination, motivation. and most of all, having God on your side and allowing God to direct you through all your decision, you have made it through all the obstacles, potholes, setbacks, detours & mountains that was in your way, you are where you were wanting to be. You've lost some things, some people through the process, but you have gained much more. A better relationship & trust in God, friends, and love ones that are going in the same direction as you, and people that push you to be the greatest that you can be. People who want to see you successful, instead of a failure. You've found a better, stronger, more knowledgeable and wiser you that have more of a dept understanding. The great thing is, all the tools and keys you've gained along the way can be used to keep you moving in the direction that you desire to go, to move you even closer to your destination in life. You have the road map that you've created to your success, and one day you may have the opportunity to direct someone else in the right direction and be of help to them. Breath, relax & thank God for the help He has given you to go from where you were to where you are now. There is much more learning, developing and maturing to do, but you are on the right path to your destiny and there is no better place to be then in God – in your divine destiny. Through each chapter of this book, there were many opportunities to ask the question of, <u>WHAT'S STOPPING YOU?</u> And to answer the question of, *what's stopping you?* Is the answer – nothing, nothing is stopping you from progressing, nothing is stopping you from achieving, nothing is stopping you from starting and becoming successful in the business that you desire to have? Whatever you feel is stopping you, is just a part of your imagination and is a defense mechanism to keep you from moving forward. So don't let the only thing that has the ability to stop you, be yourself. Continue to want the best for yourself, as well as for others.

I pray that this book have been encouraging to you and a helpful tool that you could add to your collections. I pray that this book was able to add guidance in some areas of your life that seemed to be rough periods, where you just needed some encouragement. I ask God to bless the reader of this book and give them the direction that's needed to move them to their <u>Divine Destiny</u> and turn them from that <u>I Can't</u> to the <u>I Can</u> attitude. In Jesus name.

Spiritual Reflection

SPIRITUAL REFLECTION

SCRIPTURE

Romans 8:31 – What then shall we say in response to these things? If God is for us, who can be against us?

REFLECTION

We have God Almighty on our side, the ultimate Creator, the ultimate Authority, has prepared you for the work that He has called you for, you can do <u>ALL</u> things through Christ who strengthens you.

I want to thank the one and only God, Jehovah Jireh, among many other names, for providing me with the wisdom and the desire to write this 1st book. Without God nothing is possible, both with God all things are possible. Thank you Lord, it's not me, but you and you deserve all the Glory, the entire honor, and all the Praise.

Thank You Lord

Printed in the United States
By Bookmasters